ANDREW LLOYD WEBBER'S

BIG NOTE PIANO

The PHANTOM of the OPERA

ISBN 0-7935-1656-0

HAL•LEONARD
CORPORATION
7777 W. BLUEMOUND RD. P.O. BOX 13819 MILWAUKEE, WI 53213

ALL I ASK OF YOU

Music by ANDREW LLOYD WEBBER
Lyrics by CHARLES HART
Additional Lyrics by RICHARD STILGOE

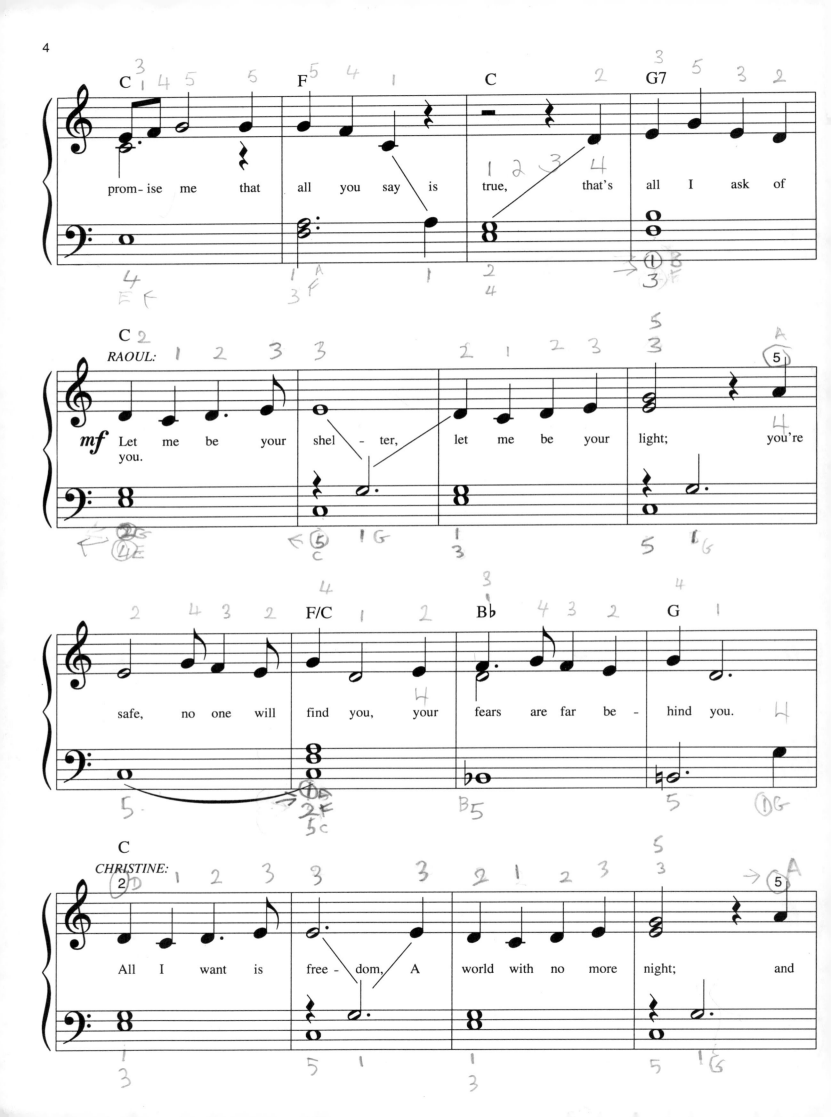

4

ANGEL OF MUSIC

Music by ANDREW LLOYD WEBBER
Lyrics by CHARLES HART
Additional Lyrics by RICHARD STILGOE

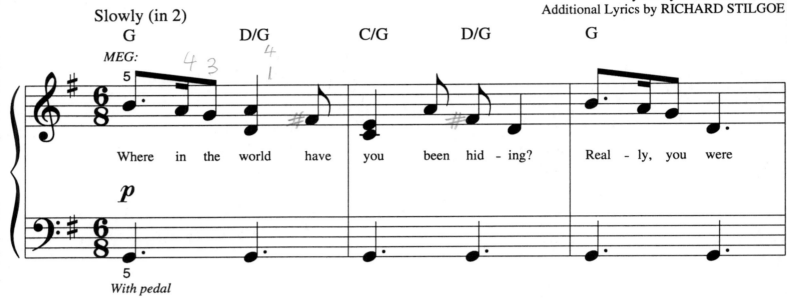

Where in the world have you been hid - ing? Real - ly, you were

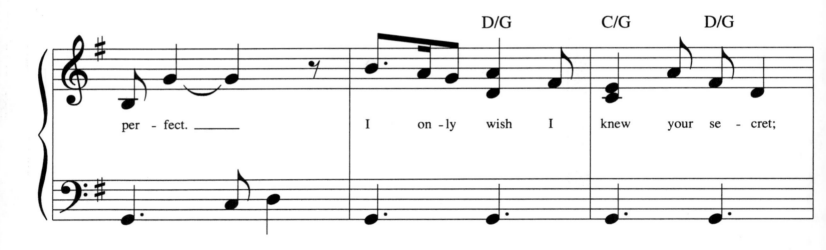

per - fect. _____ I on -ly wish I knew your se - cret;

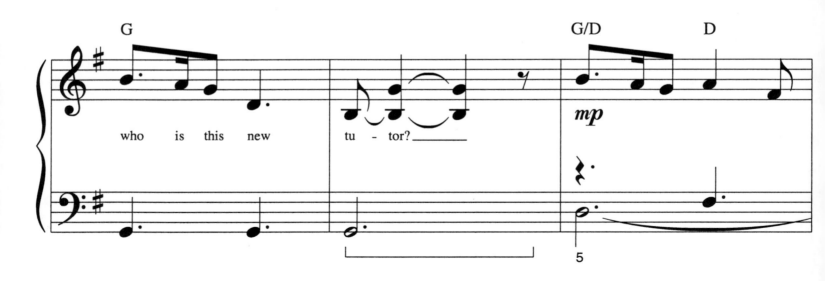

who is this new tu - tor? _____

10

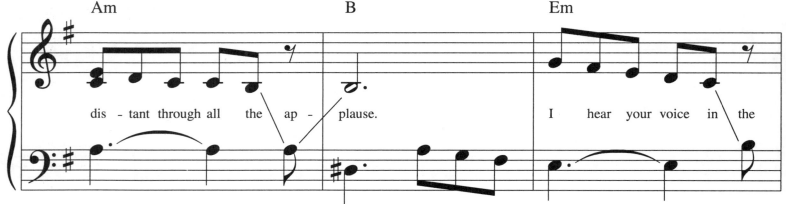

Moderately fast

MASQUERADE

Music by ANDREW LLOYD WEBBER
Lyrics by CHARLES HART
Additional Lyrics by RICHARD STILGOE

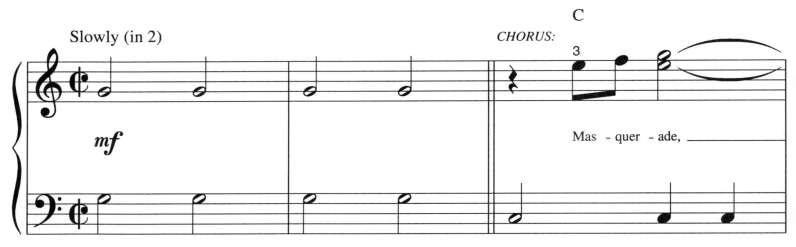

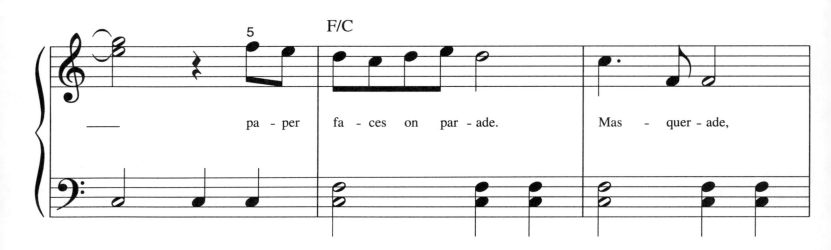

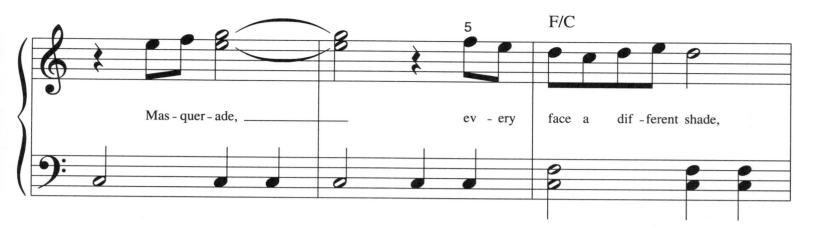

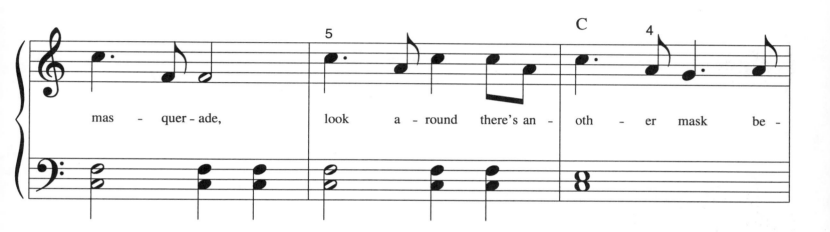

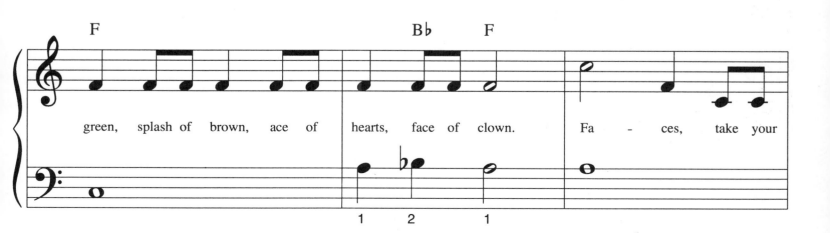

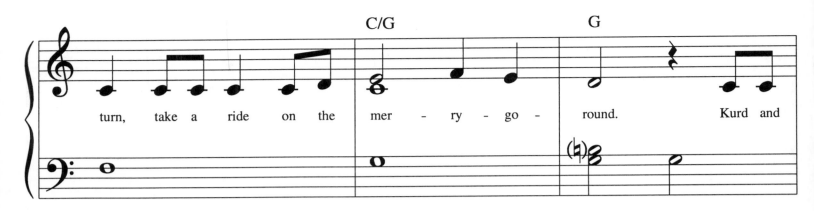

grin - ning yel - lows, spin - ning reds. Mas - quer - ade,

take your fill, let the spec - ta - cle as - tound you.

Mas - quer - ade, _____ burn - ing glan - ces, turn - ing heads,

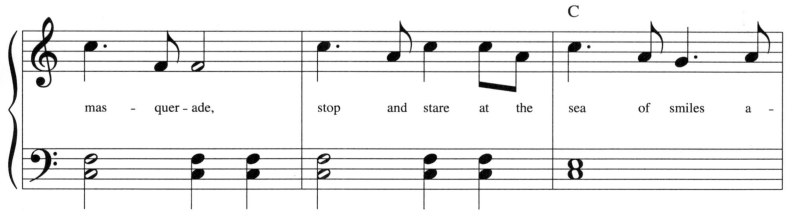

mas - quer - ade, stop and stare at the sea of smiles a -

18

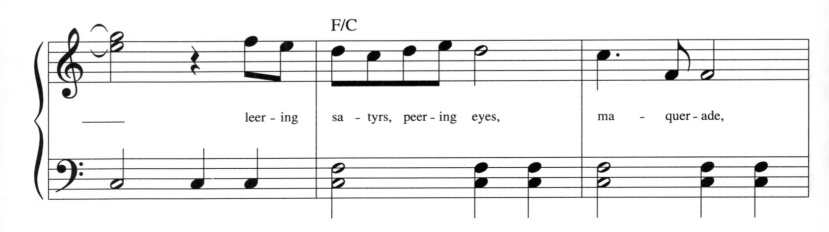

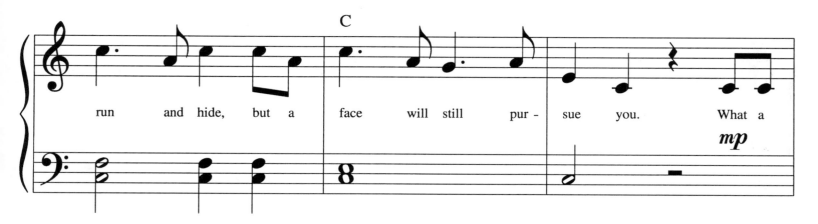

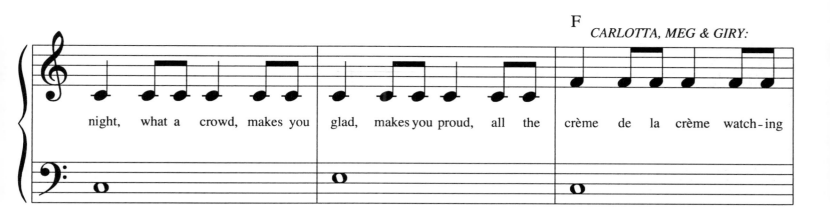

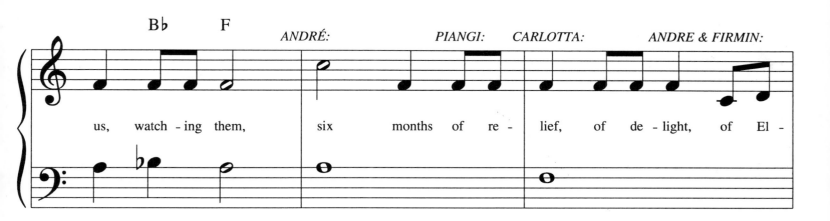

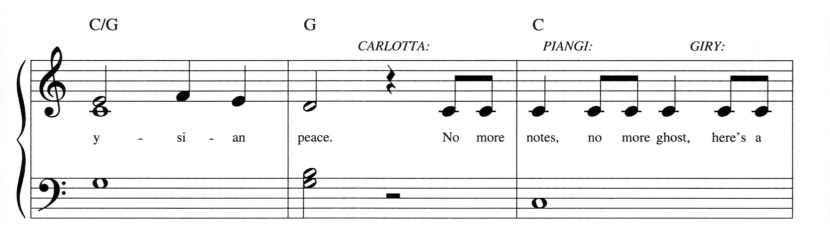

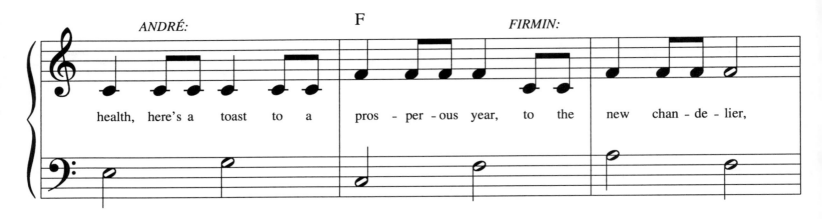

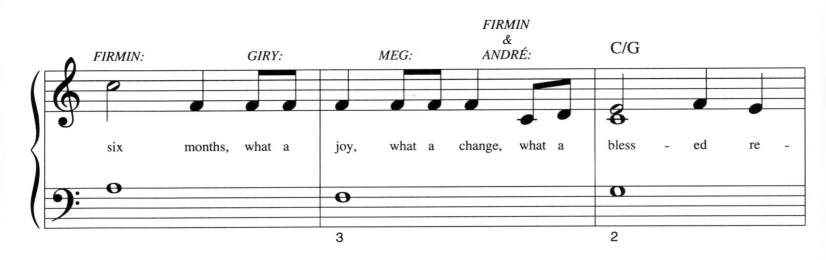

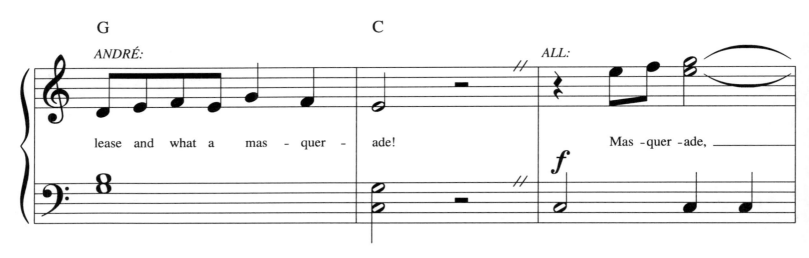

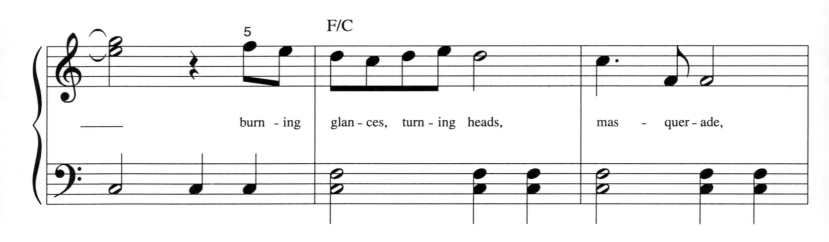

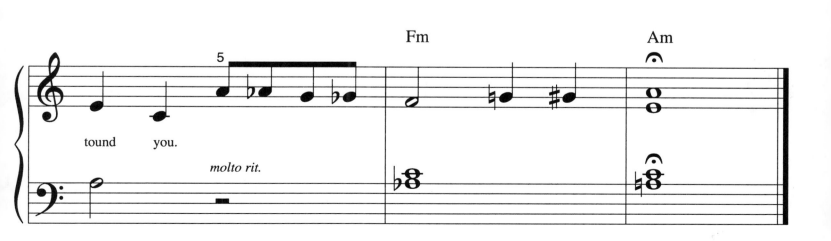

THE MUSIC OF THE NIGHT

Music by ANDREW LLOYD WEBBER
Lyrics by CHARLES HART
Additional Lyrics by RICHARD STILGOE

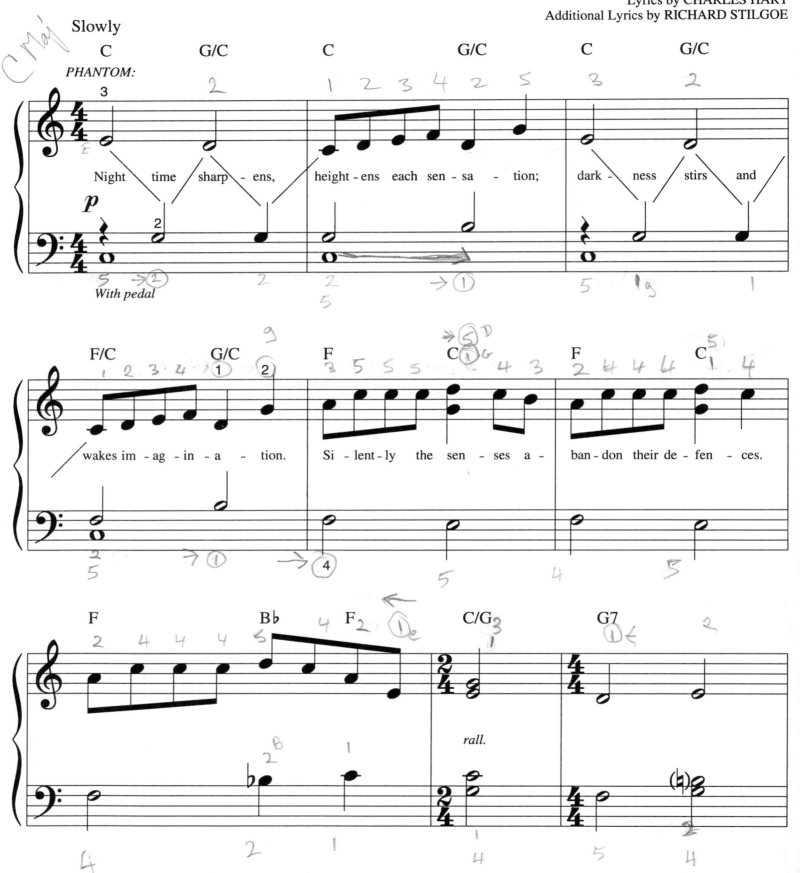

night.

You a - lone can make my song take flight, help me make the mu - sic of the

night.

PRIMA DONNA

Music by ANDREW LLOYD WEBBER
Lyrics by CHARLES HART
Additional Lyrics by RICHARD STILGOE

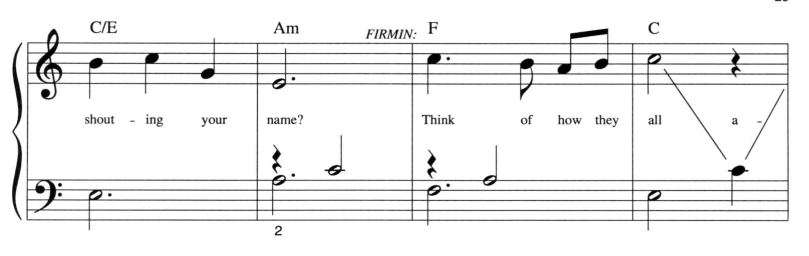

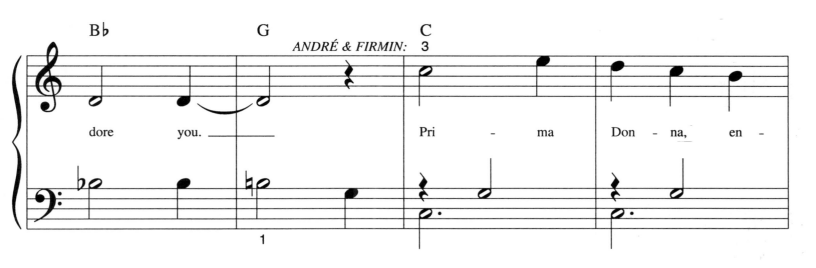

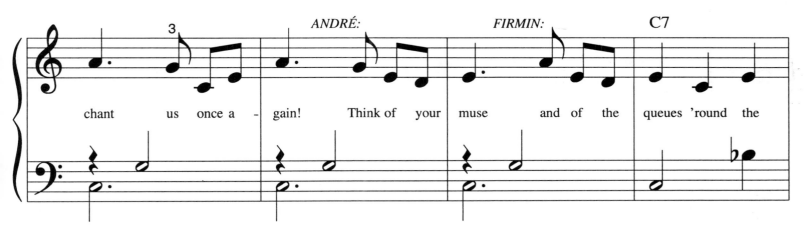

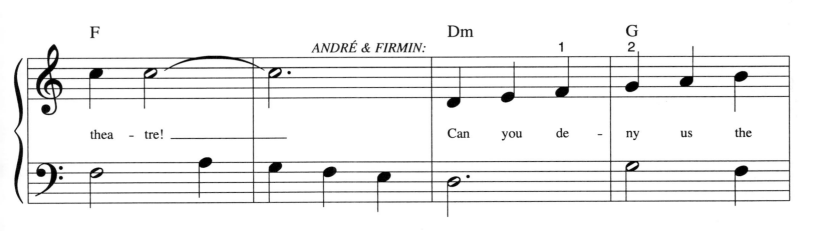

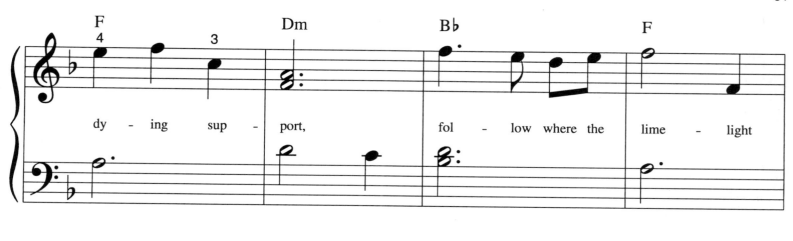

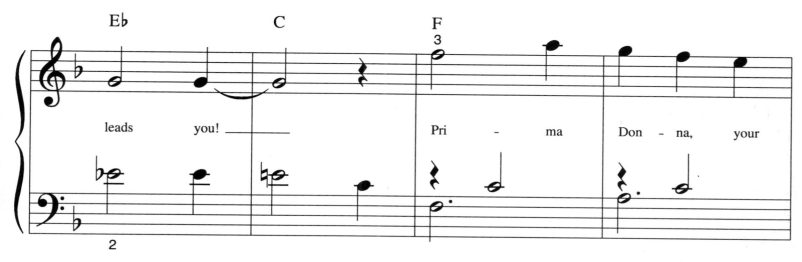

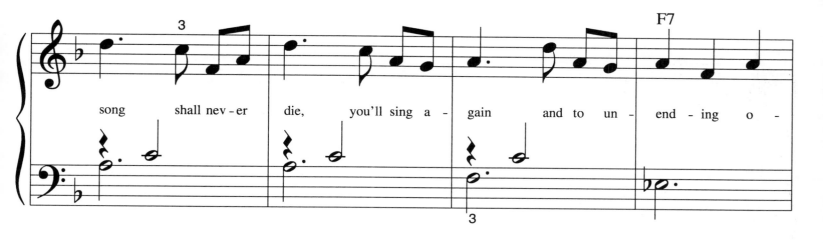

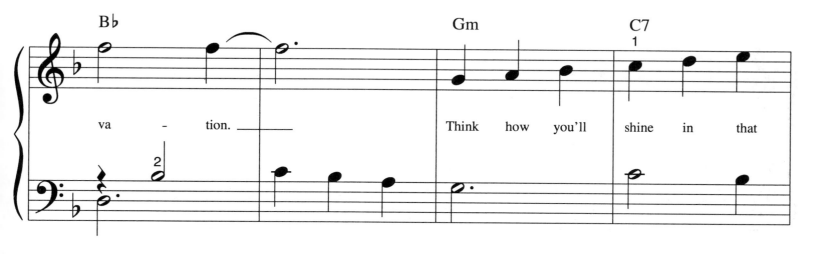

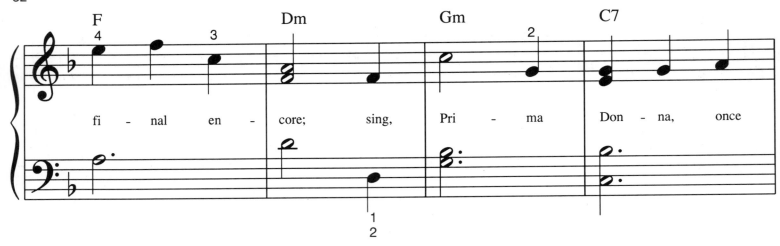

fi - nal en - core; sing, Pri - ma Don - na, once

optional cut to

ANDRÉ & FIRMIN:

more! Who'd be - lieve a di - va hap -py to re - lieve a

cho - rus girl who's gone and slept with the pa - tron?___ Raoul and the soub - rette en -

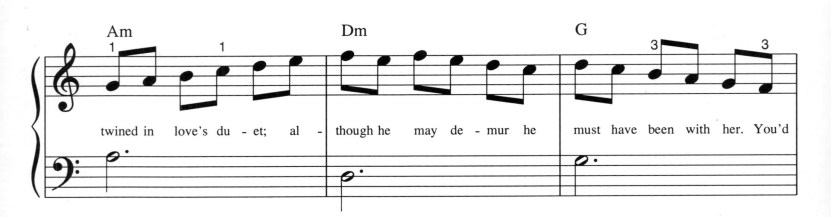

twined in love's du - et; al - though he may de - mur he must have been with her. You'd

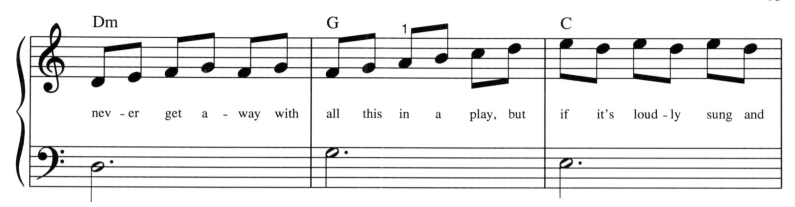

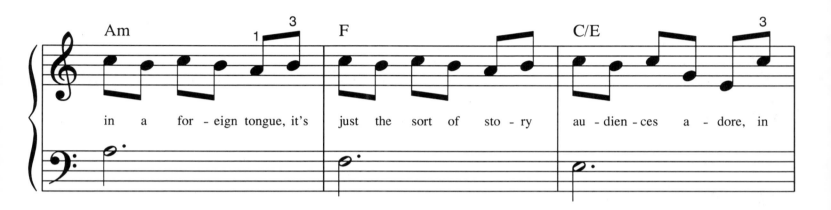

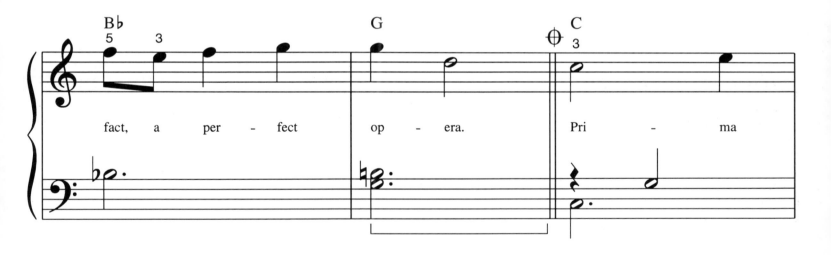

34

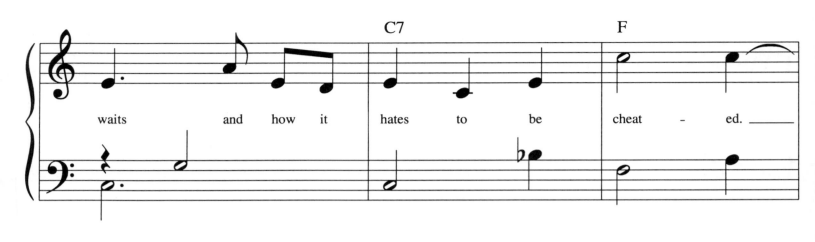

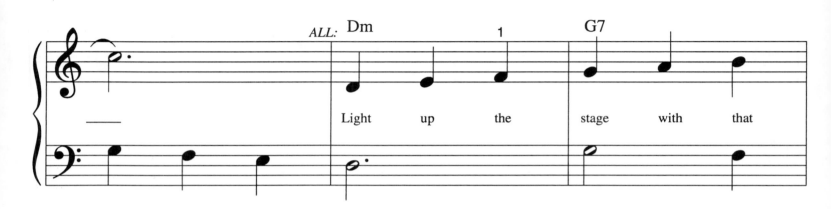

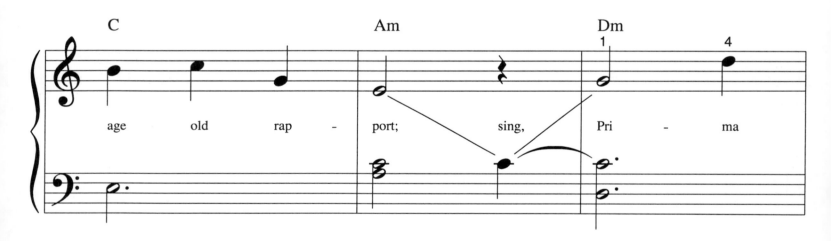

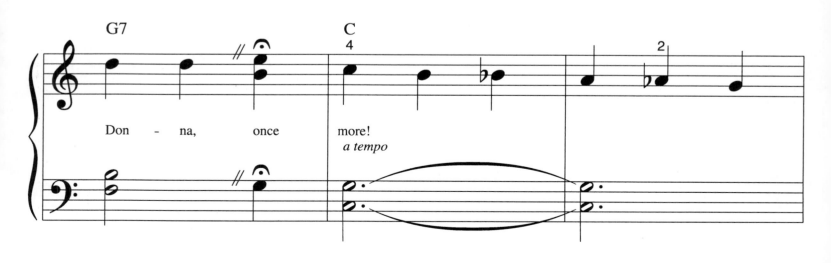

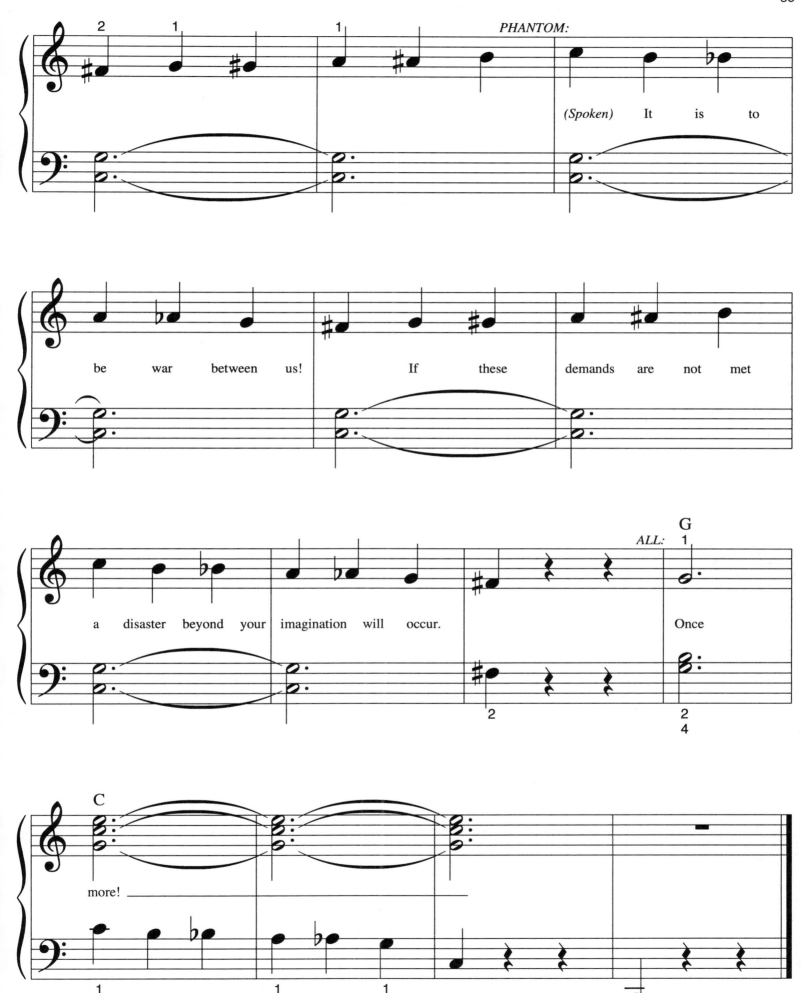

THE PHANTOM OF THE OPERA

Music by ANDREW LLOYD WEBBER
Lyrics by CHARLES HART
Additional Lyrics by RICHARD STILGOE
and MIKE BATT

37

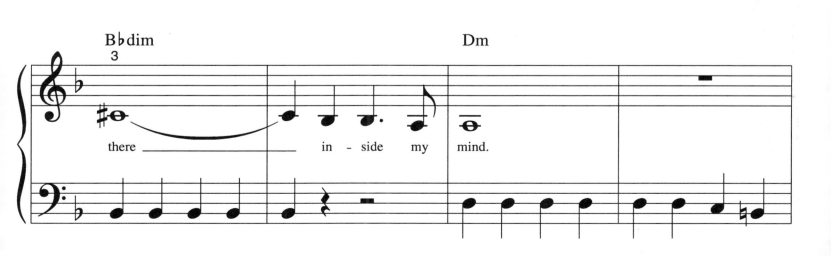

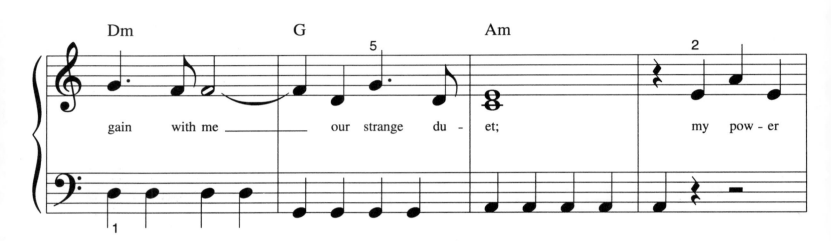

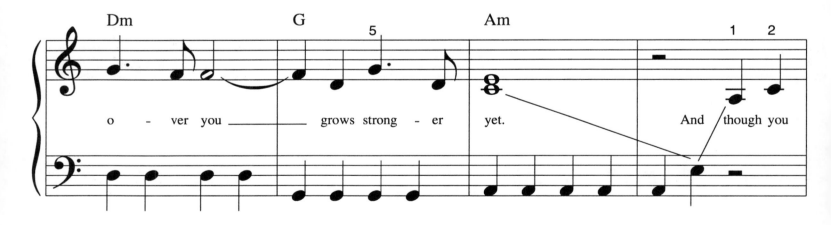

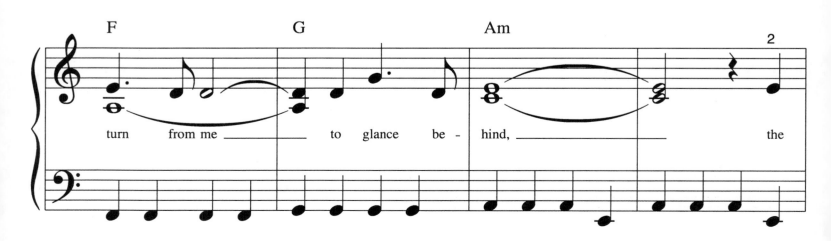

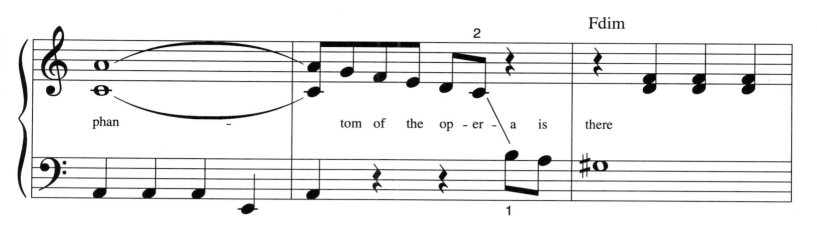

phan - tom of the op - er - a is there

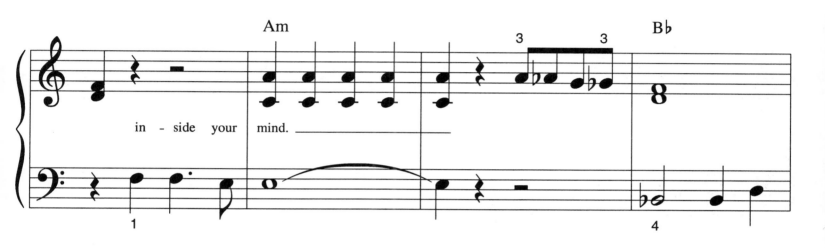

in - side your mind.

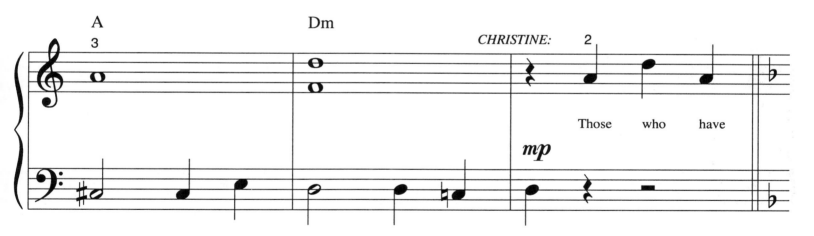

CHRISTINE:

Those who have

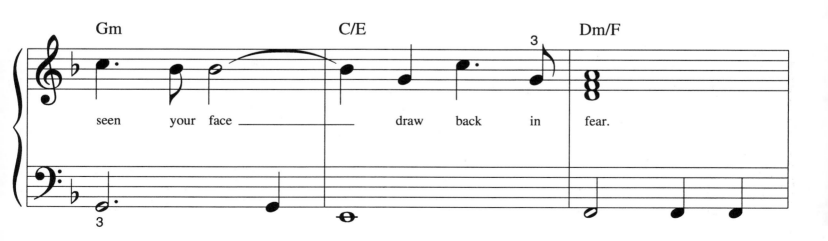

seen your face draw back in fear.

40

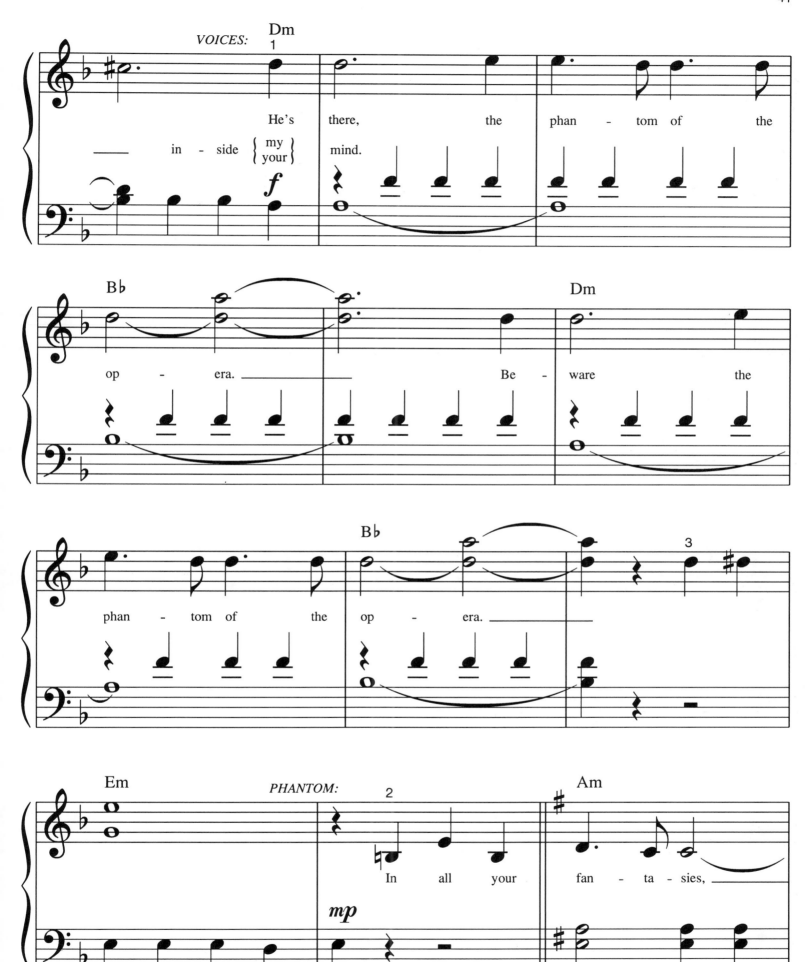

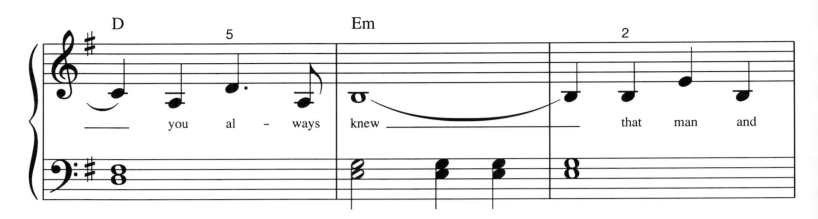

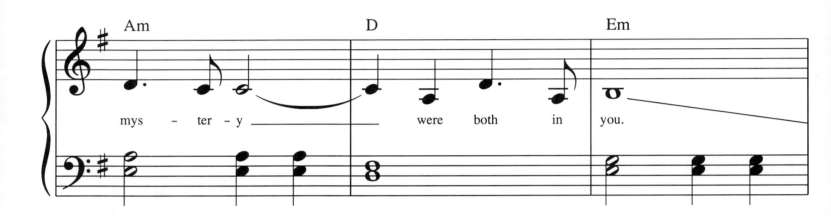

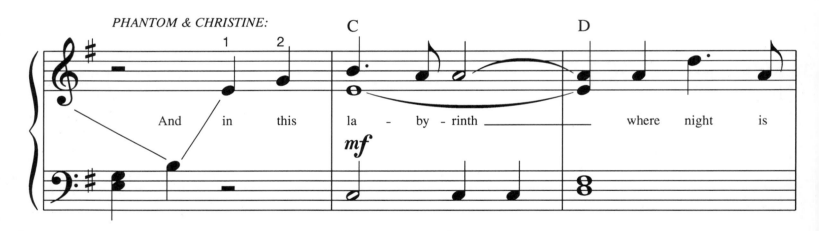

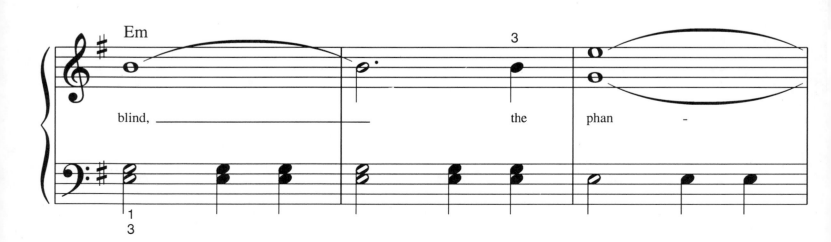

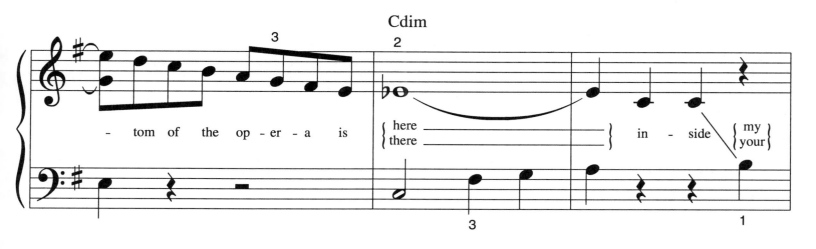

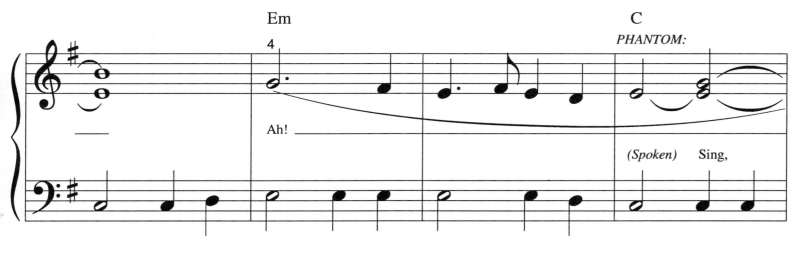

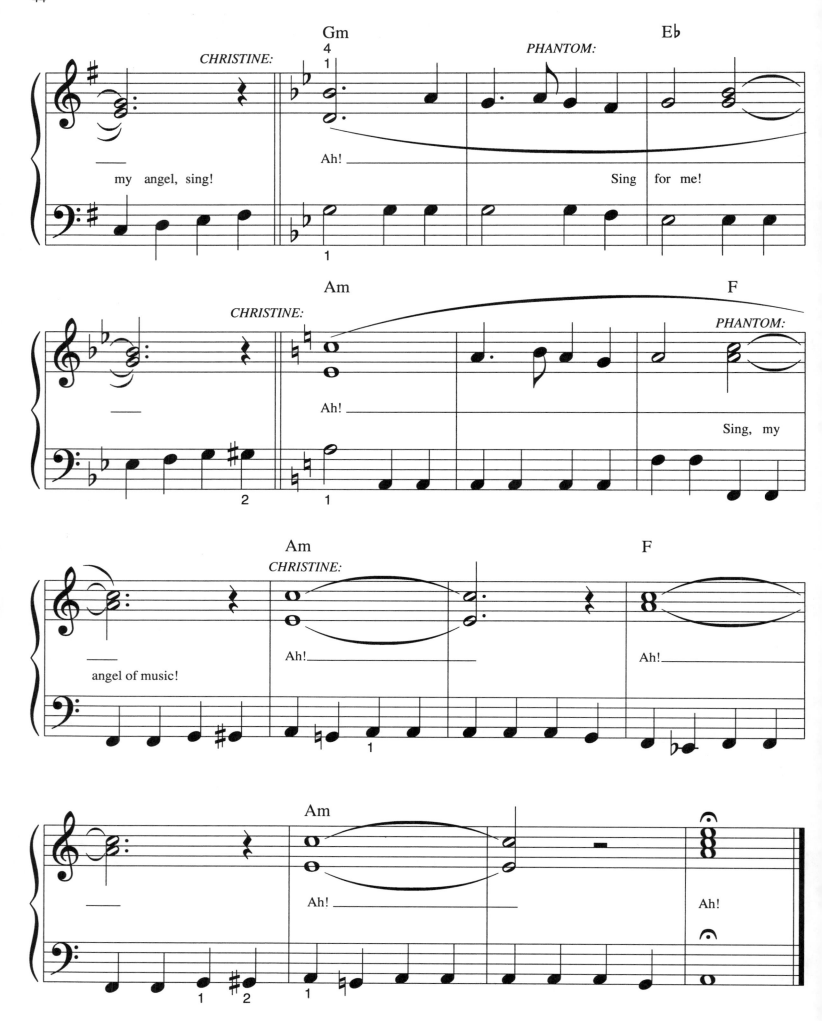

THE POINT OF NO RETURN

Music by ANDREW LLOYD WEBBER
Lyrics by CHARLES HART
Additional Lyrics by RICHARD STILGOE

46

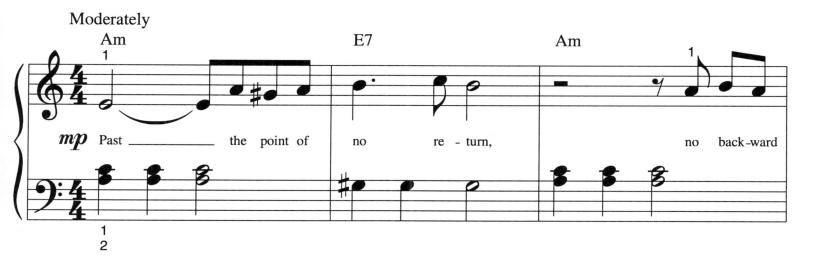

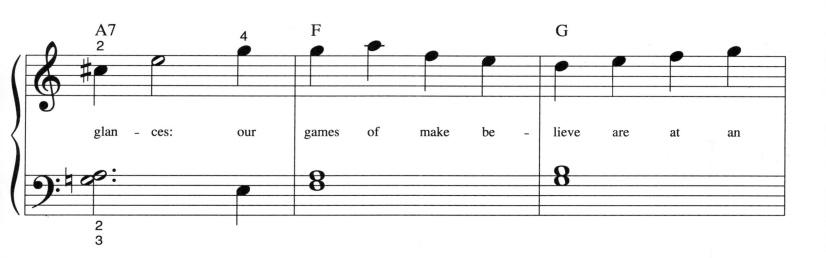

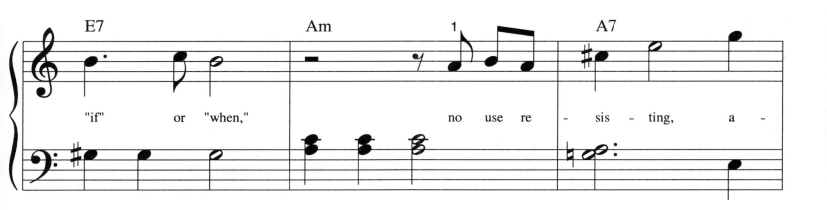

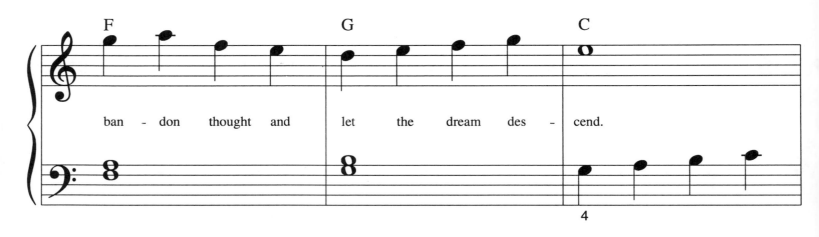

ban - don thought and let the dream des - cend.

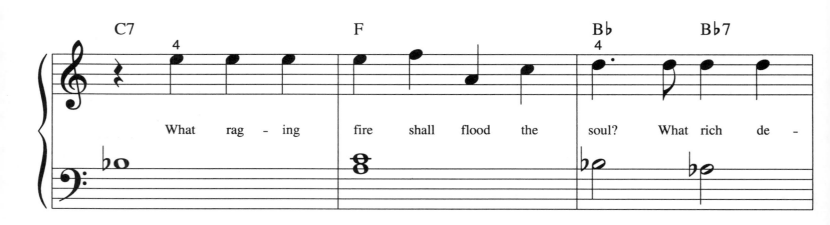

What rag - ing fire shall flood the soul? What rich de -

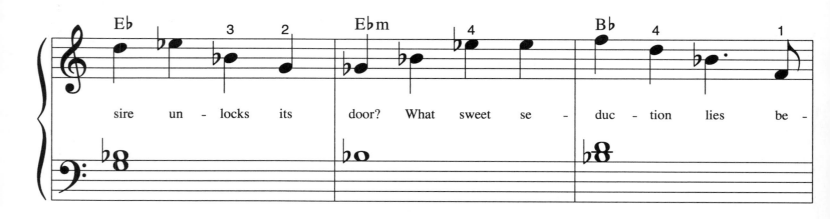

sire un - locks its door? What sweet se - duc - tion lies be -

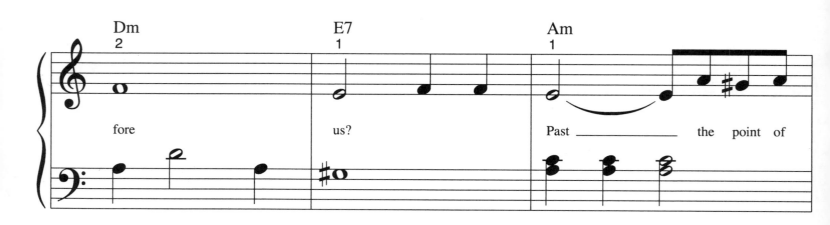

fore us? Past _____ the point of

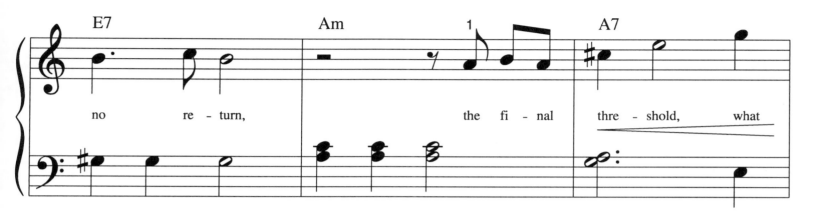

no re - turn, the fi - nal thre - shold, what

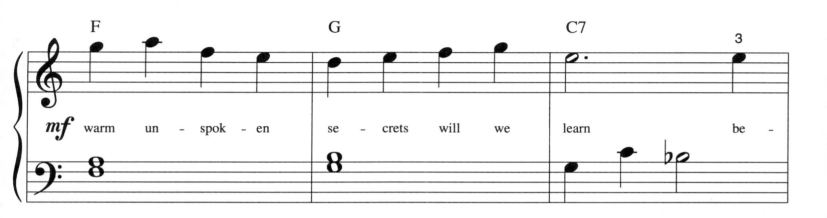

mf warm un - spok - en se - crets will we learn be -

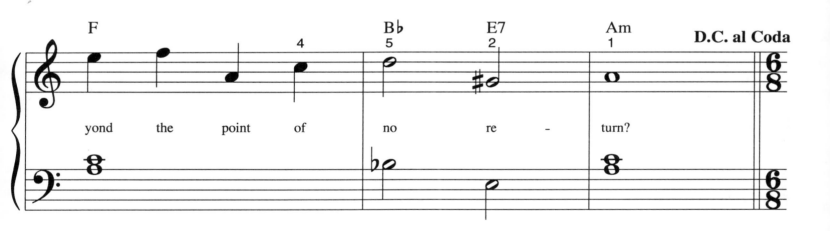

D.C. al Coda

yond the point of no re - turn?

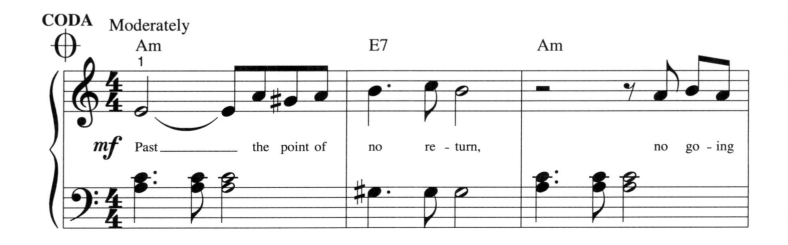

CODA Moderately

mf Past_____ the point of no re - turn, no go - ing

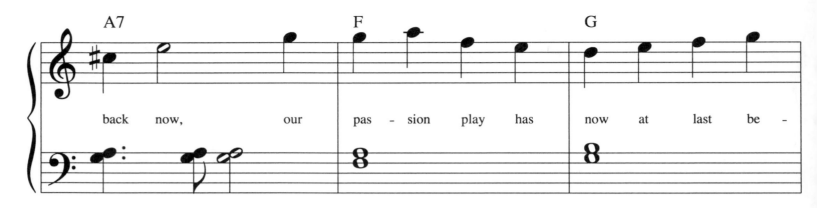

back now,   our   pas - sion play has   now   at   last   be -

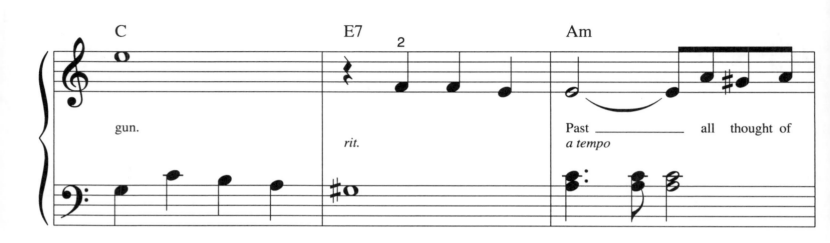

gun.   rit.   Past _____ all   thought of
                                                              a tempo

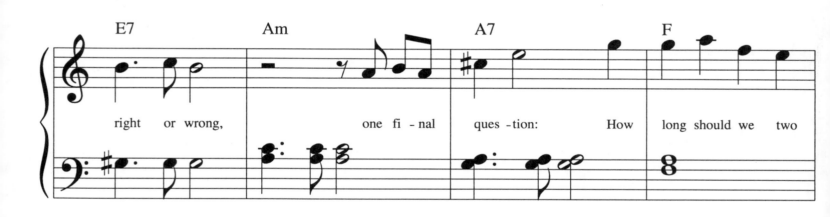

right   or wrong,   one fi - nal   ques -tion: How   long should we   two

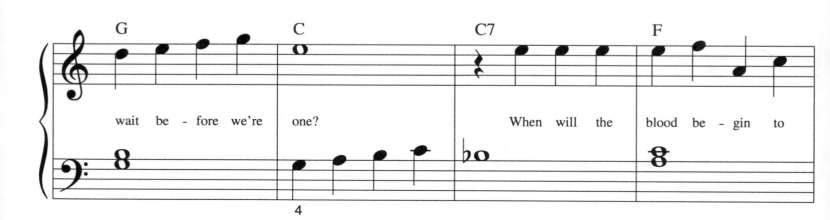

wait be - fore we're   one?   When will the   blood be - gin   to

51

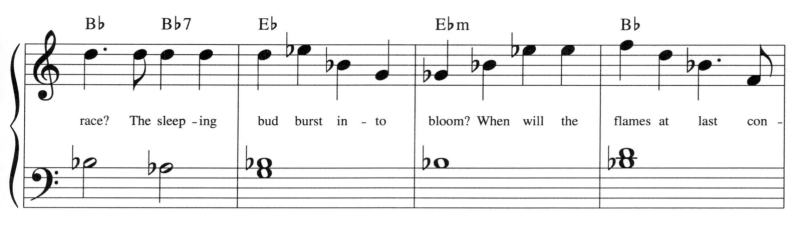

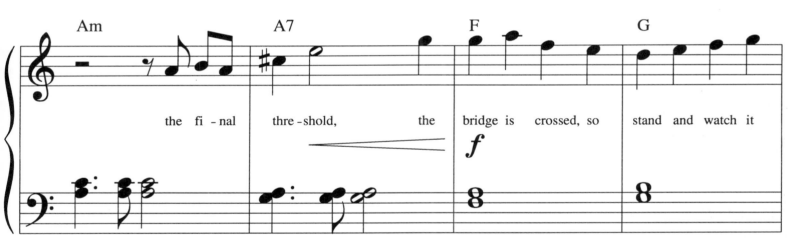

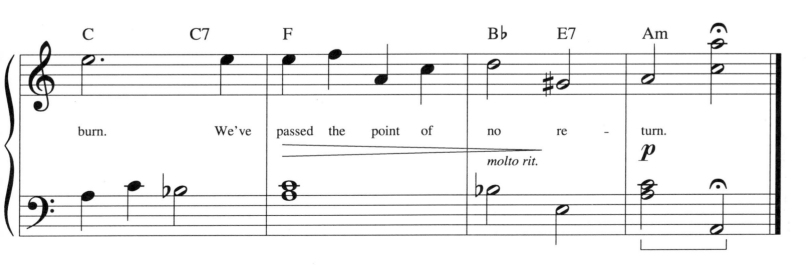

THINK OF ME

Music by ANDREW LLOYD WEBBER
Lyrics by CHARLES HART
Additional Lyrics by RICHARD STILGOE

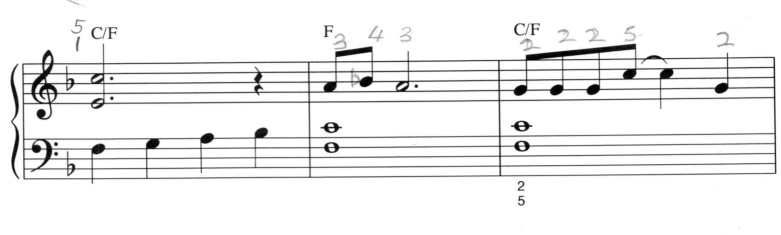

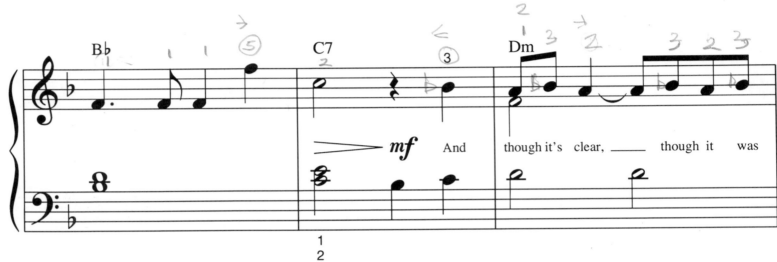

And though it's clear, _____ though it was

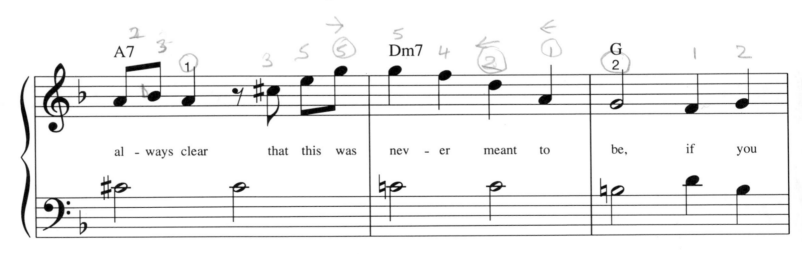

al - ways clear that this was nev - er meant to be, if you

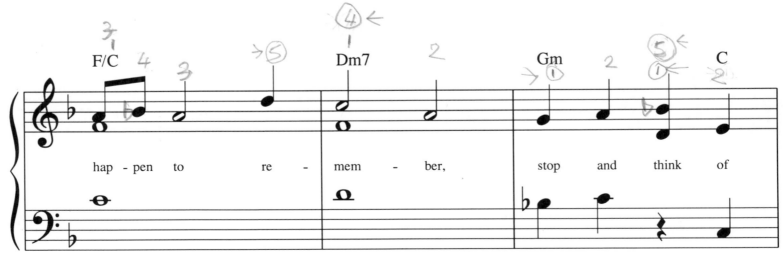

hap - pen to re - mem - ber, stop and think of

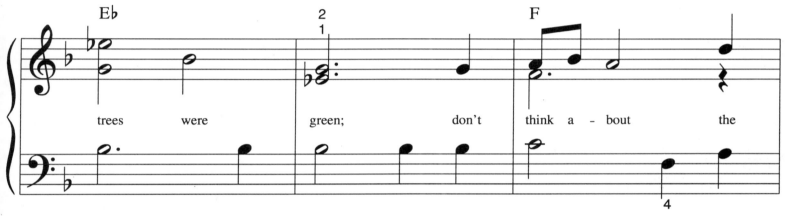

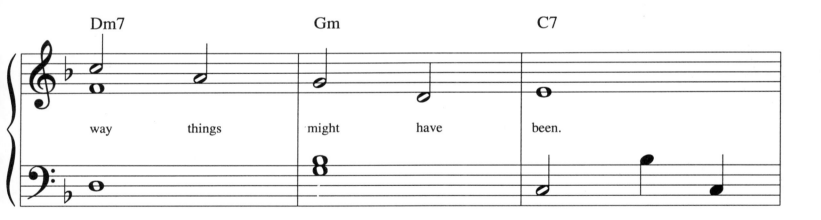

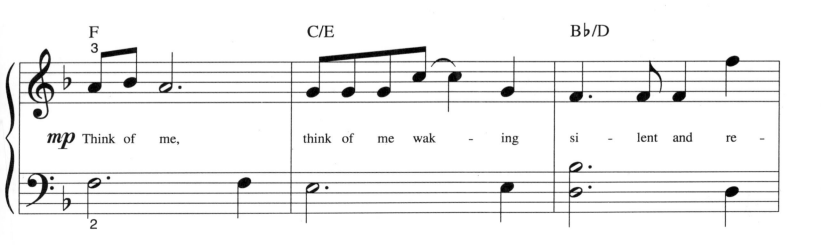

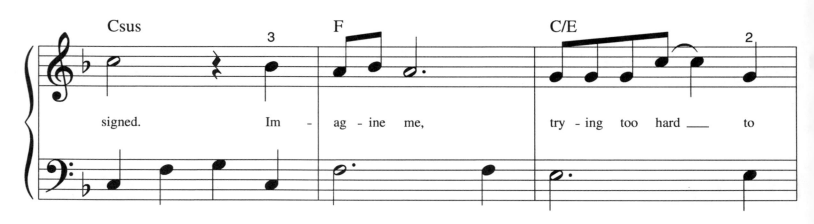

signed.   Im - ag - ine me,   try - ing too hard ___ to

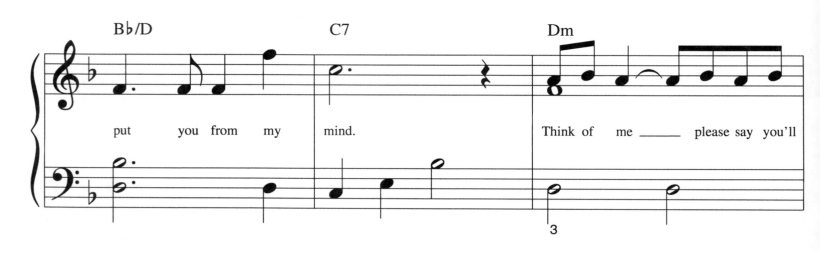

put   you from   my   mind.   Think of   me ___ please say you'll

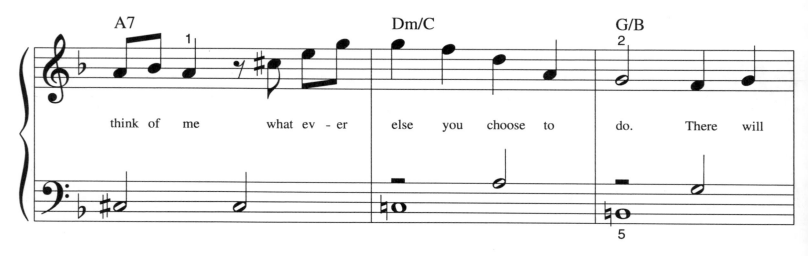

think of   me   what ev - er   else   you   choose to   do.   There   will

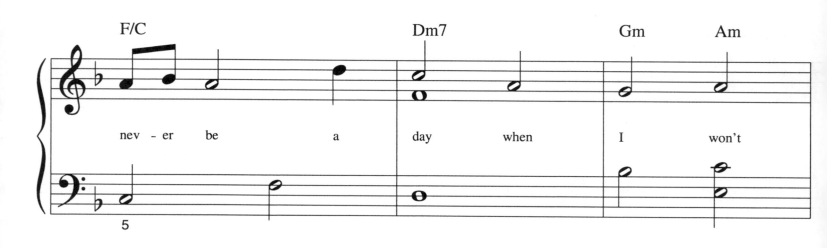

nev - er   be   a   day   when   I   won't

WISHING YOU WERE SOMEHOW HERE AGAIN

Music by ANDREW LLOYD WEBBER
Lyrics by CHARLES HART
Additional Lyrics by RICHARD STILGOE

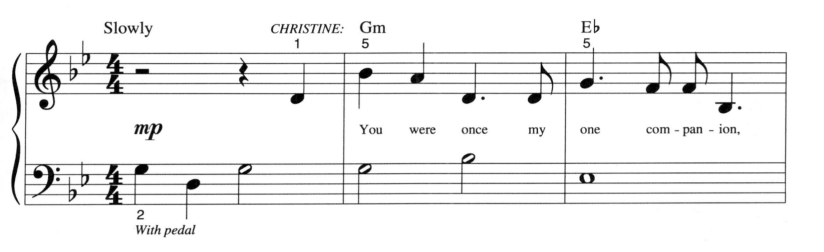

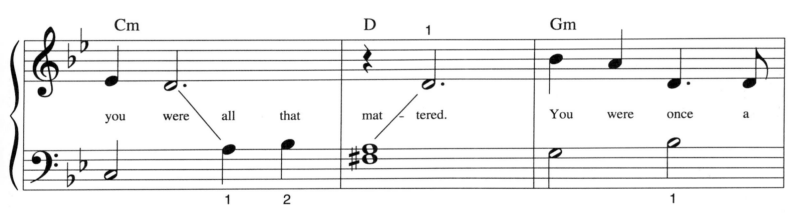

60

61

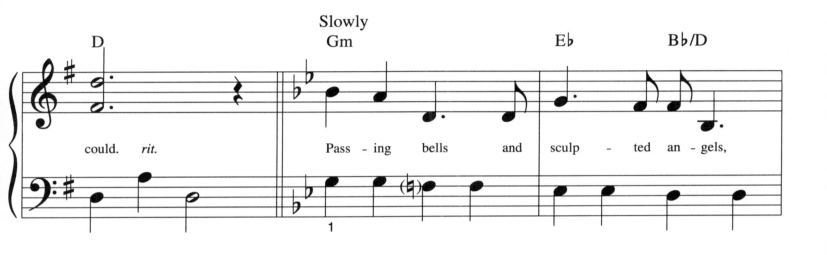

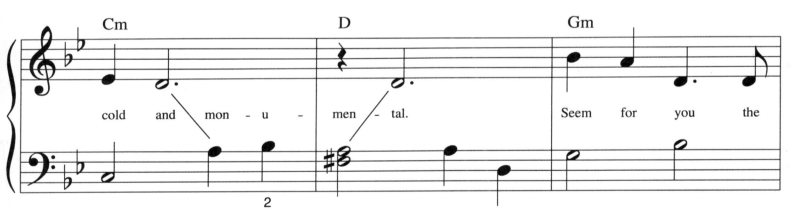

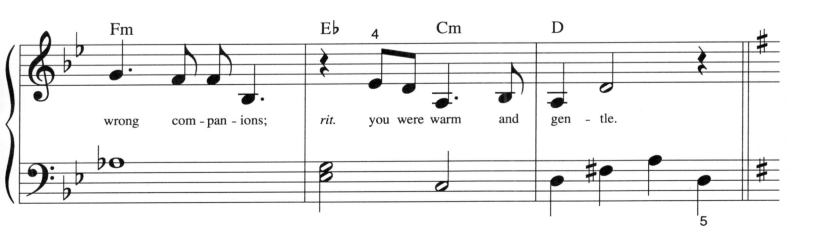